Prophetic Finance

The Christian's 12 Step Guide to Creating Wealth with the Spoken Word

Dr. Linda Sharon Sanders

U.S. Copyright Number: TXu001078078/02/06/2003

ISBN-10: 0692332537:
ISBN-13: 978-0692332535

DEDICATION

To:

My Daddy God
His Son, Jesus
The Holy Spirit

Thank you for being such wonderful Counselors,
Overseers, Best Friends,

My Everything!

My Family

Last, but not Least -

My Grandchildren

I love you guys!

&

The Late Bishop George D. Lee III

The Cathedral of the Holy Spirit at Living Word
Christian Center, Augusta, Georgia

CONTENTS

PROPHETIC FINANCE

ACKNOWLEDGMENTS

Unless Otherwise Indicated, Bible Quotations are taken from the Amplified Bible, copyright 1965, 1987 by The Zondervan Corporation. The Amplified New Testament copyright 1958, 1987 by the Lockman Foundation. Used by permission.

Introduction

"My people are destroyed for lack of knowledge; because you have rejected knowledge, I will also reject you that you shall be no priest to Me; seeing that you have forgotten the law of your God, I will also forget your children." Hosea 4:6

My father was a wonderful man, one day the Lord really blessed him from an accident at his job. I was nineteen years old. Overnight we were catapulted from poverty to a season of blessing. None of us knew Jesus as our Lord. In a matter of three years, the blessing was virtually all gone. Two years later, my father passed away suddenly, leaving us in a mountain of debt. Financial advice he had received and followed left our family full of uncertainty about our financial future. It led us to a twenty year battle with the woes of poverty once again.

This book tells of my initial experience in prophetic finance and details the wisdom God gave me over a period of three years. These events led me into a season of prosperity and blessing.

Many Christians have done all within their power to walk in the blessing that the Bible says belongs to them, but to no avail. So many of us have tithed, given offerings and nothing has manifested. It is at this point some people give up on God and declare the teaching on prosperity is not true. We know what the Bible says about our prosperity and we wonder when it will be our turn to experience prosperity.

This is my story and it contains the wisdom the Holy Spirit revealed to me regarding the lack of the blessing in my life. Ephesians says all things work together for those who love God and who are called according to His purpose. All of the biblical principles outlined in this book will work together to create your financial harvest. Step by step, line upon line, precept upon precept.

These principles will work for anyone who will put them to work because they are based on the truth of the Word of God. I thank God every day His promises of prosperity are not based on my educational background, my station in life, my race, my gender, or even my age. Jesus said it is the truth that will make you free, and it is God's truth on prosperity that will set you on the road to prosperity for your soul and pocketbook.

III John 2 says "Beloved, I pray that you may prosper in every way and [that your body] may keep well, even as [I know] your soul keeps well and prospers. You have to first believe that God wants your finances to prosper, even as He is prospering your soul by the Word of God.

There are some streams of thought in the Body of Christ today preaching and teaching that wanting to be prosperous is evil and should not be sought after by the Christian, not even in prayer. The Bible states the love of money is the root of all evil, but money itself is neutral. As I will later outline in this book, money is simply a method of exchange; a tool to get things done – God's things. God wants us to be blessed so we can bless others, support the Gospel, support our families, and leave an inheritance to our children's children.

The mindset that says prosperity is the mark of a carnal Christian has a religious mindset such as the Pharisees and the Sadducees had when they did not want Jesus to heal on the Sabbath.

I was able to bless more people, support more ministries, and lay the foundation for my grandchildren to have wealth since God had prospered me, but this is just the beginning. There are still more realms of supernatural finance to be experienced, taught and passed on.

The keys contained in this book, working together, put you in a position to receive from God. This is what this book is about. I know you have heard all of the faith teachings about prosperity. I had also heard. What I heard was true, but God wants to add to the revelation we in the Body of Christ have received. He wants to fine tune the wisdom He has already given us through His Word and bring us into the good land He has prepared for all of His children.

My friend, God is not a respecter of persons. I believe the steps I have discussed in this book will work for whosoever will do them, and do them in faith and obedience to God's word. The reason it will work is because they are based on the truth of God's Word.

God's Word never fails, and God declares In Isaiah 55:11 His Word will not return to Him void. Apply the Word to every part of your life, including your finances and it will produce a financial harvest in your life!

Chapter One
In the Beginning

At one point in my life I was a Psychology major and it's just my nature to be curious about how things work and to be curious about the root cause of people's behavior, situations, failures and successes. As I thought I was just about to finish this book, the Holy Spirit instructed me one morning. He said, "You need to go back to the beginning."

I knew immediately what He was saying. It is completely like God to cause me to write the beginning at the end. God wants us to know the root causes of the things going on in our lives, not just the effects, so we don't repeat them.

Here is a cold, hard fact: We would not be suffering sickness, pain, grief, sin, lack or poverty if it were not for the Fall of Adam. Adam had "it going on" as today's teenagers would say. God had provided everything for him.

8And the Lord planted a garden toward the east, in Eden [delight] and there He put the man whom He had formed [constituted].

9And out of the ground the Lord God made to grow every tree that is pleasant to the sight or to be desired-good, suitable, pleasant for food; the tree of life also in the center of the garden, and the tree of the knowledge of good and evil and blessing and calamity.

[10]Now a river went out of Eden to water the garden; from there it divided and became four river heads

[15]And the Lord God took the man and put him in the Garden of Eden to tend and guard and keep it. **Genesis 2:8-10, 15**

[28]And God blessed them and said to them, Be fruitful, multiply, and fill the earth, and subdue it [using the vast resources in the service of God and man]; and have dominion over the fish of the sea, the birds of the air, and over every living creature that moves upon the earth.

[29]And God said, See, I have given you every plant yielding seed that is on the face of all the land and every tree with seed in its fruit; you shall have them for food.

[30]And to all the animals on the earth and to every bird of the air and to everything in which there is the breath of life-I have given every green plant for food. And it was so. **Genesis 2:28-30**

Adam had his every desire met in the garden. He had a beautiful wife; he had the finest cuisine that God could provide; he had an ocean view; he had control over all of it and best of all, he had God as his best friend.

It is my personal opinion that God did not want Adam, the one He created for fellowship, to be tied up doing other stuff. However, He did give Adam something minor to do so he would be not become bored, but he would have a sense of purposefulness. He instructed Adam to tend and guard the Garden, not to work it. It was all there for him. All Adam had to do was a little upkeep. Adam was living a life of true prosperity! But what went wrong?

Everything was perfect until the Fall. You could say that after the Fall of Adam, everything fell apart. Look what happened after Adam and Eve disobeyed God by eating of the Tree of the Knowledge of Good and Evil:

[17] And to Adam He said, because you have listened and given heed to the voice of your wife and have eaten of the tree of which I commanded you, saying, You shall not eat of it, the ground is under a curse because of you; in sorrow and toil shall you eat [of the fruits] of it all the days of your life.

[18] Thorns and thistles shall it bring forth for you, and you shall eat the plant of the field.

[19] In the sweat of your face shall you eat bread until you return to the ground, for out of it you were taken; for dust you are and to dust you shall return.

[23] Therefore the Lord God sent him forth from the Garden of Eden to till the ground from which he was taken. ***Genesis 3:17-19, 23***

Some of you may say, "What's wrong with a little more information?" Well, you ever heard of what we sometimes say in our generation, "maybe that was a little bit too much information?" I can not substantiate this from the Scriptures, but sometimes we don't need to know everything, we just need to trust God and the commandments that He gives us.

We are descendants of Adam, and believe it or not, we are all trying to get back to that place in the garden. This is the place where all our needs are met; we were not sick or grieved in spirit; and our relationships were good and perfect. Additionally, it appeared that Adam had that place in his heart where only God could touch and cause to be filled by continuous communion with Him.

If you are experiencing poverty and lack today, it is because of the Fall of Adam. But thank God, after pronouncing the punishments for the serpent and curses for Adam and Eve's disobedience, God declared immediately to Satan that He would send forth a Remedy:

And I will put enmity between you and the woman, and between your offspring and her Offspring; He will bruise and tread your head underfoot, and you will lie in wait and bruise His heel. **Genesis 3:15**

This is the first reference of the Savior to come in the Bible, God's Son Jesus Christ! God declared to Adam and Eve that in the fullness of time, He would send forth His Son. Through Jesus' death on the Cross, He would reverse every curse that had to come because of Adam's disobedience. Praise God for our Savior!

Chapter Two
Jesus Died for Your Prosperity

The thief comes only in order to steal and kill and destroy. I came that they might have life, and have it in abundance (to the full, till it overflows). **John 10:10**

It is so interesting that our currency in the United States has the words "In God We Trust" printed on the front, but the average Christian shuns the idea of being wealthy. We spend enormous hours every day working a job that we hate so that we might obtain as much money as we can.

I believe that most Christians are like this because of religious teaching. This teaching glorifies being poor as some kind of testament to their love for Christ. I believe this attitude is rooted in receiving salvation for works.

There are some in the Body of Christ which say: "If I could just suffer enough, I'll get to heaven one day." However, Ephesians 2:10 says:

"For we are God's [own] handiwork (His workmanship), recreated in Christ Jesus, [born anew] that we may do those good works which God predestined (planned beforehand) for us [taking paths which He prepared ahead of time], that we should walk in them [living the good life which He prearranged and made ready for us to live].

God prepared and prearranged for us to live the good life through His Son Jesus Christ. How? Through His death on the Cross, in exchange for our sin, we obtain righteousness; in exchange for sickness, we obtain health; in exchange for our poverty, we obtain wealth.

The Fall of Adam produced a curse that was three-fold: sickness, poverty and spiritual death or separation from God.

Genesis 3:17-18 says:

[17]"And to Adam He said, Because you have listened and given heed to the voice of your wife and have eaten of the tree of which I commanded you, saying, You shall not eat of it, the ground is under a curse because of you; in sorrow and toil shall you eat [of the fruits] of it all the days of your life."
[18]Thorns also and thistles shall it bring forth for you, and you shall eat the plants of the field.

It was at this point that all suffering, pain and misery entered the world, including poverty. Adam's union with God and his place of prosperity were all destroyed in one single act of disobedience. Adam was sentenced to provide for himself from that point onward.

[23]Therefore the Lord God sent him forth from the Garden of Eden to till of Eden to till the ground from which he

was taken.

[24]So [God] drove out the man; and He placed at the east of the Garden of Eden the cherubim and a flaming sword which turned every way, to keep and guard the way to the tree of life. **Genesis 3:23-24**

The thorns and thistles mentioned in Genesis 3:18 are symbolic of poverty. Isn't it interesting that a crown of thorns was placed on Jesus' head just before He was hung on the Cross? A crown of thorns, in the form of a circle was pressed upon the scalp of Jesus. This resulted in additional, but critical bleeding to our Savior.

And weaving a crown of thorns, they put it on His head and put a reed (staff) in His right hand. And kneeling before Him, they made sport of Him, saying "Hail (greetings, good health to You, long life to You), King of the Jews! **Matthew 27:29**

Every place where Jesus shed His blood was and still is a point symbolic of our redemption.

[3]He was despised and rejected and forsaken by men, a Man of sorrows and pains, and acquainted with grief and sickness; and like One from Whom men hide their faces He was despised, and we did not appreciate His worth or have any esteem for Him.

[4]Surely He has borne our griefs (sicknesses, weaknesses, and distresses) and carried our sorrows and pains [of punishment], yet we [ignorantly] considered Him stricken, smitten, and afflicted by God [as if with leprosy].

[5]But He was wounded for our transgressions, He was bruised for our guilt and iniquities, the chastisement [needful to obtain] peace and well-being for us was upon

Him, and with the stripes [that wounded Him] we are healed and made whole. **Isaiah 53:3-5**

These scriptures describe the totality of Jesus' suffering for us, so that we could be made whole. The word "whole" is translated "raphah." In the Hebrew it means to mend, to cure or (cause to) heal, or repair thoroughly. The shed blood of Jesus has provided everything for us, including healing in our finances.

Jesus truly sacrificed Himself so that we could be whole in every area. If you are not fully persuaded, then please meditate on the following scripture:

For you are becoming progressively acquainted with and recognizing more strongly and clearly the grace of our Lord Jesus Christ that though He was [so very] rich, yet for your sakes He became [so very] poor, in order that by His poverty you might become enriched [abundantly supplied]. **II Corinthians 8:9**

Jesus' death on the Cross reversed all of mankind's poverty. It is up to us as believers to go forward in faith and receive our inheritance. We must proceed knowing that God has already given us the power, the anointing to get wealth. Jesus paid the price and shed His precious blood for our prosperity.

Chapter Three
Believe

But without faith it is impossible to please and be satisfactory to Him. For whoever would come near to God must [necessarily] believe that God exists and that He is the rewarder of those who earnestly and diligently seek Him [out]. **Hebrews 11:6**

Unless you believe what the Word of God says about your prosperity, you can never expect or depend on God to intervene in the area of your finances.

Believing the Word of God to be your final authority in life is crucial to receiving anything from God. The Word of God declares in *Numbers 23:19*:

God is not a man, that He should tell or act a lie, neither the son of man, that He should feel repentance or compunction [for what He has promised]. Has He said and shall He not do it? Or has he spoken and shall He not make it good?

The promises of God are unchangeable. Man may declare and promise, and then change his mind, but not God – when it comes to His Word, He changes not.

This is why His Word is the basis of everything to the Christian. Based on the promises of the Word of God, we come into salvation; we believe that our sins have been forgiven; we receive healing. As we act on His Word, we receive the prosperity that it promises us as believers.

So then faith in the Word of God enables us to believe, and then supports and feeds our faith in God, enabling us to seek Him for our needs.

So faith comes by hearing [what is told], and what is heard comes by the preaching [of the message that came from the lips] of Christ (the Messiah Himself). **Romans 10:17**

Let me reiterate, believing God for anything is easy when you receive the Word of God as final authority in the earth and in your life.

When you fully embrace the Word of God on prosperity and wealth and not what the world thinks, not what your family thinks, and not what the religious mindset thinks, you can then take the Word and create wealth with it.

If you are a Christian, and you disbelieve God's word on prosperity, consider the consequences. Israel disbelieved God after He so gloriously brought them out of Egypt. If they had believed the promises of God, it would have taken them only eleven days to get to their promise land. Instead, Israel wondered in the Wilderness forty years until God made certain that a new generation would be born that would believe Him.

[22]Because all those men who have seen My glory and My [miraculous] signs which I performed in Egypt and in the wilderness, yet have tested and proved Me these ten times and have not heeded My voice.

[23]Surely they shall not see the land which I swore to give

to their fathers; nor shall any who provoked, (spurned, despised) Me see it. **Numbers 14:22-23**

Truly this is the divine comment about unbelief. Israel had faith to come out of Egypt, which is a type of the world, but they did not have faith to enter into their promised land. God even makes reference to the ten miraculous events that hardened and then softened Pharaoh's heart. Afterwards, he told Moses to just go and take the Israelites with him. I guess you could say that God was just a little bit miffed. Receiving Christ is the truest of prosperity and if you are not a Christian and want to receive Him today, repeat this prayer:

Unless you first receive Christ as your Personal Savior, everything that I outline in this book will not make sense to you.

The Bible declares in *Isaiah 55:8-9*:

[8]For My thoughts are not your thoughts, neither are your ways My Ways says the Lord.
[9]For as the heavens are higher than the earth, so are My ways higher than your ways and My thoughts higher than your thoughts.

If you are a sinner and you picked up this book, the first step to believing the Word of God is to become a believer.

The Scripture declares in *I Corinthians 2:14*:

But the natural, non-spiritual man does not accept or welcome or admit into his heart the gifts and teachings and revelations of the Spirit of God, for they are folly (meaningless nonsense) to him; and he is incapable of knowing them [of progressively recognizing, understanding, and becoming better acquainted with them] because they are spiritually discerned and estimated and appreciated.

You are a spirit, you have a soul, and you live in a body.

I Thessalonians 5:23
And may the God of peace Himself sanctify you through and through [separate you from profane things, make you pure and wholly consecrated to God]; and may your spirit and soul and body be preserved sound and complete and found] blameless at the coming of our Lord Jesus Christ (the Messiah).

After you make Jesus the Lord of your life, your spirit now dead, becomes alive and is regenerated. Why?

It is so that you can see, understand, and comprehend God. The Bible says that a veil is taken from your eyes when you turn to God.

II Corinthians 3:14-16
[14]*In fact, their minds were grown hard and calloused [they had become dull and had lost the power of understanding]; for until this present day, when the Old Testament (the old covenant) is being read, that same veil still lies [on their hearts], not being lifted [to reveal] that in Christ it is made void and done away.*
[15]*Yes, down to this [very] day whenever Moses is read, a veil lies upon their minds and hearts.*
[16]*But whenever a person turns [in repentance] to the Lord, the veil is stripped off and taken away.*

Whether Jew or Greek, after receiving Jesus Christ as your Personal Savior, you will begin to understand the Word of God and be enabled to receive its truth –

including the truth about divine prosperity.

Romans 10:9 says:

[9] *"Because if you acknowledge and confess with your lips that Jesus is Lord and in your heart believe (adhere to, trust in, and rely on the truth) that God raised Him from the dead, you will be saved.*

[13] *For whosoever shall be call upon the name of the Lord shall be saved.* **Romans 10:9, 13**

So it's very easy to enter into the Kingdom of God and give your life to His Son, Jesus Christ!

Repeat this prayer:

Lord, I come to You now, in the name of Jesus.

I am a sinner. I ask You to forgive me of my sins and cleanse me of my unrighteousness.

I believe in my heart that Jesus Christ is the Son of God.

I believe He was raised from the dead for my justification.

I believe that He paid the price for my sins.

I am calling upon His Name – the Name of Jesus –

I do believe with my heart, and I confess Jesus now as my Lord!

I believe now that my name in the Lamb's Book of Life

Therefore I am saved!

Thank you, Father!

If you prayed this prayer and sincerely meant it in your heart, you are saved! Not only is your name written in the Lamb's Book of Life, but now you can begin to hear and comprehend God – Your Father, and the Creator of the Universe!

For the sinner, this prayer provides prosperity for your soul and it is the first step to creating wealth with the spoken Word.

Chapter Four
Seek Ye First the Kingdom of God

[28]But if God so clothes the grass in the field, which is alive today, and tomorrow is thrown into the furnace, how much more will He clothe you, O you [people] of little faith.

[29]And you, do not seek [by meditating and reasoning to inquire into] what you are to eat and what you are to drink; nor be of anxious (troubled) mind [unsettled, excited, worried, and in suspense]:

[30]For all the pagan world is [greedily] seeking these things, and your Father knows that you need them.

[31]Only aim at and strive for and seek His kingdom, and all these things shall be supplied to you also. **Luke 12:27-31**

In the last verse of these scriptures, the word "seek" in the Greek means to desire, to worship, to inquire, to require, as requiring God as your vital necessity.

As you may have already heard, especially if you have been in Christian circles, God is all-knowing, He is ever present in every place, and He is all-powerful. Wow, what a combination!

You may be saying, "What does this have to do with my financial harvest?" It has everything to do with your financial harvest.

I am in no way suggesting that we seek God for His

blessings only. What I am suggesting is that you as a believer will have to humble yourself before Him in worship and praise. Praise Him for Who He is and for what He has done for us in the plan of redemption and even regarding our financial condition. I heard a minister on television say "God knows where all the gold is." Why consult anyone about your finances without consulting Him first?

If you are a Christian, it is vital that you seek God and His kingdom first. Another parallel scripture in *Matthew 6:33* says:

But seek (aim at and strive after) first all of His kingdom and His righteousness (His way of doing and being right), and then all these things taken together will be given you besides.

One of the reasons I believe the Holy Spirit has this verse of scripture in the Bible is because He knows that after we do everything in our own power to get wealth, He wants to remind us to seek first the Kingdom of God.

In other words, Jesus was saying seek after God first before you do anything else about your financial situation. Add this to your understanding of being and doing right; and this will put you in position to receive all that you need from your heavenly Father.

I know some Christians right now that want the blessing of God on their life, but their ways are not right. They depend on manipulation: making someone feel sorry for them, outright begging, and even some good storytelling to get their financial needs met. Then they wonder why it is that they are not experiencing the blessing of God. This is what sinner's do. They plot, they steal, deceive, and some even murder to get wealth.

Many of them do not know that God has provided a better way to get and keep wealth. However, the Christian must look to God. The Scripture plainly states that we as Christians must be seeking after His kingdom and His ways of doing and being right. You don't have to be perfect to receive the wealth of God, for we all sin and fall short of His glory. However, we must do our best to do what God requires, and immediately repent when we realize that we have sinned. We can only accomplish this as we continually seek Him.

God loves us so very dearly, by seeking Him first, you will build a trusting relationship with Him. In the next few chapters, I will discuss becoming rooted and grounded. Part of becoming rooted and grounded is loving God first, not money.

His goodness, His kindness, His mercy and love will cause you to require Him as your vital necessity and then motivate you to seek ye first the Kingdom of God. Everything that I expound upon in this book is critical to receiving supernatural finances from God. The most important is seeking after God. When you seek after God, He will lead you to what you need to do next to take hold of money.

II *Chronicles 31:20-21*
[20] *"Hezekiah did this throughout all Judah, and he did what was good, right, and faithful before the Lord His God.*
[21] *And every work that he began in the service of the house of God, in keeping with the law and the commandments to seek his God [inquiring of and yearning for Him], he did with all his heart, and he prospered."*

When you seek Him first, not only do you get to know Him, but He will begin to guide you in His will for your finances.

In 1996, after going through a terrible divorce and subsequent bankruptcy, I made up in my mind that I was going to really seek God with all my heart. I would hear Gloria Copeland and other ministers on television talk about spending time with God. I felt that I was missing out. I determined that I was going to seek God with all my heart. It was really the start of the beautiful relationship that I have with the Lord even to this day.

One thing that you will discover after you receive your financial harvest: nothing can take the place of Jesus in your life. You will realize that money is just a tool to get things done. Money and wealth will become very dissatisfying without the Lord Jesus Christ.

Matthew 6:25
"No one can serve two masters; for either he will hate the one and love the other, or he will stand by and be devoted to the one and despise the other and be against the other. You cannot serve God and mammon (deceitful riches, money, possessions, or whatever is trusted in).

After God blessed me financially to the place where I could buy almost anything that I wanted, I began to despise the riches. I almost wished that I did not have the money at all. But as I sought the Lord all the more, even in the midst of being blessed, He gave me balance. He filled me with His joy. There is a saying in the world, "What good is success without someone to share it with?" The same is true with finances, believe me, it is nothing without Jesus at your side.

It is very empty unless you continue your relationship with the Lord, and help those whom are in need around you.

This is why I believe that many of the rich and famous commit suicide and become alcoholics or drug addicts. Riches without a relationship with God are very, very empty.

As a matter of fact God says in **Deuteronomy 8:18** *that "you shall earnestly remember the Lord your God, for it is He Who gives you power to get wealth, that He may establish His covenant which He swore to your fathers, as it is this day."*

He also makes it very clear that if you fail to remember Him, you shall surely perish from the earth.

And if you forget the Lord your God and walk after other gods and serve them and worship them, I testify against you this day that you shall surely perish. **Deuteronomy 8:19**

It won't be God causing you to perish. It will be you trying to fill the void in your life without Him that will cause you to perish.

There is a void in your heart that only a relationship with Jesus will fill. If you try to fill it with material things like cars, furs, diamonds, cars, houses, etc., you will feel the deepest void.

So by seeking first the Kingdom of God, you get to know and fall in love with Him. He will become someone that you will not want to be without, no matter what material things you possess.

Solomon was the wisest man who ever lived on the earth. He had it all. Kings and queens came from all over the land to see him and meet with him because of his great wealth and volumes of wisdom. As God prophesied to Solomon, there has been none like him since.

But after obtaining all the wealth, all the women, all the fame, and all the recognition, he declared that the end of the matter is this:

All has been heard: the end of the matter is: Fear God [revere and worship Him, knowing that He is] and keep His commandments, for this is the whole of man [the full, original purpose of his creation, the object of God's providence, the root of character, the foundation of all happiness, the adjustment to all harmonious circumstances and conditions under the sun] and the whole [duty] for every man. ***Ecclesiastes 12:13***

This is what a man, who had everything, had to say when he summarized what was really important in life.

The Presence of God

[1]Make a joyful noise unto the Lord, all you lands!
[2]Serve the Lord with gladness! Come before His presence with singing!
[4]Enter into His gates, with thanksgiving and a thank offering and into His courts with praise! Be thankful and say Him, bless and affectionately praise His name!
[5]For the Lord is good: and His mercy and loving-kindness are everlasting, His faithfulness and truth endure to all generations. ***Psalms 100:1-2, 4-5***

As you are seeking first the Kingdom of God, and the King Himself, I want to exhort you to just get into His presence.

Verse 2 of Psalms 100 says to enter into His gates. First of all, when you are endeavoring to get into the presence of God, we all start out in the flesh. We have to make a decision that we are going to make the attempt to enter in that blessed place.

Also in that same verse it says that we enter with thanksgiving and praise. I didn't really have a good time in prayer until I bought a few compact discs over thirty years ago and began to praise God even before I began to pray. Praise inevitably leads to worship; sustained worship inevitably leads us into His presence.

The Bible says that the Father is seeking those who will worship Him in spirit and in truth. Worship allows you to access and enter into the presence of God. Instead of a labor, prayer became a joy. Some awesome things began to happen to me in my secret place.

There are many Christians who attend church, teach Sunday school, and even some Pastors and ministers who have not ever met God in the secret place. Your finances take on a new dimension when you begin to enter into the secret place. This is where you will begin to hear directly from God and intimacy with God will affect the decisions that you make in every area of your life. He says in *Isaiah 30:21:*

And your ears will hear a word behind you saying, this is the way; walk in it, when you turn to your right hand and when you turn to the left.

The following is a plan for prayer in your secret place. These steps are not written in stone, but most importantly, you must be in tune with the Spirit of God, so be open to His leading.

1. Adoration – **Daniel 4:34, 35** – *"And at the end of days [seven years], I, Nebuchadnezzar, lifted up my eyes to heaven, and my understanding and the right use of my mind returned to me; and I blessed the Most High [God] and I praised and honored and glorified Him Who lives forever."* Use the Psalms to tell God how wonderful and awesome He is.

2. Confession – **I John 1:9** – *"If we freely admit that we have sinned and confess our sins, He is faithful and just (true to his own nature and promises) and will forgive our sins [dismiss our lawlessness] and [continuously] cleanse us from all unrighteousness [everything not in conformity to His will in purpose, thought and action].* Enter into the Holy of Holies by confessing any known sin in thoughts, words, or deeds.

3. Supplication – **I Timothy 2:1, 3** –

[1]*"First of all, then I admonish and urge that petitions, prayers, intercessions, and thanksgivings be offered on behalf of all men."*
[3]*Such praying] is good and right, and [it is] pleasing and acceptable to God our Savior."*

Base your prayer requests on the Word of God by personalizing and praying the scriptures according to what you have need of in the Name of Jesus.

4.　　　Intercession – James 5:15 – "And the prayer [that is] of faith will save him who is sick, and the Lord will restore him; and if he has committed sins, he will be forgiven."

　　　Pray for others that have needs around you, and bless your enemies.

5.　　　Thanksgiving – Philippians 4:6 "Do not fret or have any anxiety about anything, but in every circumstance and in everything, by prayer and petition (definite requests), with thanksgiving, continue to make your wants, known to God." As an act of your faith, give God praise and thanksgiving for the requests that you have made of Him.

Be warned that Satan will fight you with every weapon he has when you make up in your mind that you are going to seek God and get into His presence. He will tell you that you do not have enough time. He will convince you that if you sacrifice and get up early in the morning to pray, you will not be able to stay awake at work.

If you are committed to get up early to pray, he will try to make you sleepy. Satan will do anything to keep you out of the secret place.

He knows that once you get into the Presence of God, and start communing with Him, you will begin to hear Him. When you begin to hear Him; He will lead you to many places: places of victory in your marriage, places of victory in your health, places of victory on your job, places of victory in your family, including your wealthy place.

Praying the Scriptures on Prosperity

James 4:2-3

[2] *"You are jealous and covet [what others have] and your desires go unfulfilled; [so] you become murderers. [To hate is to murder as far as your hearts are concerned].* [3]*You burn with envy and anger and are not able to obtain [the gratification, the contentment, and the happiness that you seek], so you fight and war, you do not have, because you do not ask.*

[3]*[Or] you do ask [God for them] and yet fail to receive, because you ask with wrong purpose and evil, selfish motives. Your intention is [when you get what you desire] to spend it in sensual pleasures."*

Many Christians have prayed and often wondered why their prayers are not answered, particularly in the area of prosperity. The scripture quoted above is very clear about why we don't receive answers to our requests for prosperity. Not only is God listening to our prayers, but He is also looking at our heart.

In order to avoid selfish praying, it is very important during your prayer time that you make prosperity confessions according to the Word of God. When you pray the scriptures pertaining to prosperity, there is a built in checks and balances system in the Word of God.

For instance, when you pray Luke 6:38 you should pray:

Father, I thank you that I give, and it is given unto me again, pressed down, shaken together, and men giving into my bosom. By praying you activate the giver in you, which is turn is responsible for men coming and giving into your bosom, and selfishness is eliminated.

Chapter Five
Repent of Sin and Transgression

One of the most destructive components in believing for your financial breakthrough will be sin and transgression. *Deuteronomy 28:15 says: "But if you will not obey the voice of the Lord your God, being watchful to do all His commandments and His statutes which I command you this day, then all these curses shall come upon you and overtake you."*

Sin and transgression will repel the blessings of God from your life.   Sin is disobedience to God's law. Transgression is defined as a violation of God's law.   The punishment for breaking God's holy commandments manifests threefold: poverty, sickness and spiritual death, or separation from God.   The curse of disobedience is outlined in the following verses of scripture in *Deuteronomy 28:16-20:*

[16]Cursed shall you be in the city and cursed shall you be in the field.
[17]Cursed shall be your basket and your kneading trough.
[18]Cursed shall be the fruit of your body, of your land, of the increase of your cattle and the young of your sheep.
[19]Cursed shall you be when you come in and cursed shall you be when you go out.

[20]The Lord shall send you curses, confusion, and rebuke in every enterprise to which you set your hand, until you are destroyed, perishing quickly because of the evil of your doings by which you have forsaken Me.

I think that you get the picture here. The Scripture continues to document the curse of defeat in the life of those who forsake God.

One notorious story of the consequences of one man's sin and disobedience to the lord's command is Achan.

After the victory at Jericho, the Israelites went up against the few people of Ai:

Joshua 7:4-5; 7-11
[4]So about three thousand Israelites went up there, but they fled before the men of Ai.
[5]And the men of Ai killed about thirty-six of them, for they chased them from before the gate as far as Shebarim, and slew them at the descent. And the hearts of the people melted and became as water.
[11]Israel has sinned; they have transgressed My covenant which I commanded them. They have taken some of the things devoted [for destruction]; they have stolen, and lied, and put them among their own baggage.

The lord continued to tell Joshua that this is why Israel could not stand and defeat their enemies. They took the things that were set apart for destruction and put them among their own stuff. The bottom line is that they transgressed God's covenant, and committed a trespass against the Lord.

The bottom line is that they transgressed God's covenant and committed a trespass against the Lord.

To remedy the situation, God told Joshua to have all the tribes of Israel present themselves the next morning. They came by tribes, then families, households and finally persons. It was then revealed that Achan was the one that had transgressed the Lord's commandment.

Joshua 7:16-19

[16]So Joshua rose up early in the morning and brought Israel nearby their tribes, and the tribe of Judah was taken.

[17]He brought near the family of Judah, and the family of the Zerahites was taken; and he brought near the family of Zerahites man by man, and Zabdi was taken.

[18]He brought near his household man by man, and Achan son of Carmi, the son of Zabdi, the son of Zerah, of the tribe of Judah was taken.

[19]And Joshua said unto Achan, My son, give, I pray thee, glory to the LORD God of Israel, and make confession unto him; and tell me now what thou hast done; hide it not from me.

What happened to Achan? He was stoned and his body was burned with fire. This seemingly small indiscretion cost him his life!

Now we are under the Dispensation of Grace and we are talking about sin and how it relates to your finances. If you commit a sin, I doubt very seriously that you will be stoned and your body burned immediately after you sin. But the Bible declares that the wages of sin is death.

For the wages which sin pays is death, but the [bountiful] free gift of God is eternal life through (in union with) Jesus Christ our Lord. ***Romans 6:23***

Yes, sin and transgression, continued and not atoned or repented for will pay you big time. It will pay you in sorrow, in pain, in poverty, lack and sickness. Sin and transgression will always cause the heavens to close over you. The pleasure of sin, though very brief, is not worth the pain that it will cost you.

Just to be clear, I am talking to you as a Christian, not as a sinner. God will do whatever it takes to try and get the Christian back in alignment with Him and His Word. He is the ultimate Father and will discipline us because of His love.

Hebrews 12:5-6
⁵And have you [completely] forgotten the divine word of appeal and encouragement in which you are reasoned with and addressed as sons? My son, do not think lightly or scorn to submit to the correction and discipline of the Lord, nor lose courage and give up and faint when you are reproved or corrected by Him;
⁶For the Lord corrects and disciplines everyone whom He loves, and He punishes, even scourges, every son whom He accepts and welcomes to His heart and cherishes.

There was a time in my life where I was living in an area of transgression against the Lord and nothing spiritually that I would do: pray, tithe or fast would change the fact that I was living under a "closed heaven."

Deuteronomy 28:23 says "the heavens over your head shall be brass and the earth under you shall be iron."

Even after I corrected my area of transgression against the Lord, the spirit of debt, lack and poverty continued to linger in my life.

The Holy Spirit later revealed to me that this was the result of a curse. Curses are always a result of sin. Sin acts as an assassin to your financial harvest. You must purpose in your heart that you will not transgress God's laws.

Romans 8:2 *declares "For the law of the Spirit of life [which is] in Christ Jesus [the law of our new being] has freed me from the law of sin and of death."*

If you are in sin, repent before God, and ask for His grace to stop. He will provide the strength that you need to turn from sin. Don't let sin rule and reign in your mortal body. Jesus Christ paid the price for your redemption, spiritually, physically, mentally and financially. Refuse to follow the path that the devil has outlined for you.

John 10:10 says: *"Satan comes to kill, steal and destroy; I came that you might have life and have it more abundantly."*

Know that God wants you to be blessed and live outside the fruits that sin can bring into your life. Satan wants to see to it the blessing will be repelled from you. Close the door of the door of the devil's destruction through sin in your life. You will be one step closer to receiving your financial harvest.

Chapter Six
Get Rooted and Grounded

One of the first things that I thanked God for when He brought forth my financial harvest was the trying financial times. I even thought that it was strange that I felt this way. I had gone through some very tough years. My late pastor would say that I was not able to "pay attention." But with many tears, I thanked the Lord for those times. Then I understood what God told the Hebrews:

Deuteronomy 8:1-3
¹All the commandments which I command you this day you shall be watchful to do, that you may live and multiply and go in and possess the land which the Lord swore to give to your fathers.
²And you shall earnestly remember all the way which the Lord Your God led you these forty years in the wilderness, to humble you and to prove you, to know what was in your [mind and] heart, whether you would keep His commandments or not.
³And He humbled you and allowed you to hunger and fed you with manna, which you did not know nor did your fathers know, that He might make you recognize and know that man does not live by bread only, but man live by every word that proceeds out of the mouth of the Lord.

God is in the blessing business. There are three things that could affect you if you are not rooted and grounded in the lord:

1.   You could become puffed up with pride.

2.   You could forget the Lord.

3.   You could spend the wealth on ungodly pursuits

I John 2:16

For all that is in the world-the lust of the flesh [craving for sensual gratification] and the lust of the eyes [greedy longings of the mind] and the pride of life [assurance in one's own resources or in the stability of earthly things]- these do not come from the Father, but are from the world [itself].

The scripture above makes no distinction between rich or poor. You could be poor and still indulge in the "lusts of the flesh." In our society, it is very easy to shift your desires from the Kingdom of God because of all the distractions around you.

As Christians, when you set your affections on the things of the world, you run the risk of alienating yourself from God by setting your ultimate values and pursuits on the things of the world. The number one thing that God is concerned with is your soul.

Matthew 16:26

For what will it profit a man if he gain the whole world and forfeits his life [his blessed life in the Kingdom of God] Or what would a man give as an exchange for his [blessed] life [in the kingdom of God]?

Not everyone is spiritually mature enough to enter into their promise land. God allows us to be in the wilderness only to prepare us for the blessing. Should you turn from Him once He blesses you, it is His promise that you will perish.

Deuteronomy 8:7-11; 19

[7]For the Lord your God is bringing you into a good land, a land of brooks and water, of fountains and springs, flowing forth in valleys and hills;

[8]A land of wheat and barley, and vines and fig trees and pomegranates, a land of olive trees and honey;

[9]A land in which you shall eat food without shortage and lack nothing in it; a land whose stones are iron and out of whose hills you can dig copper.

[10]When you have eaten and are full, then you shall bless the Lord your God for all the good land which He has given you.

[11]Beware that you do not forget the Lord your God by not keeping His precepts, and His statutes which I command you today.

[19]And if you forget the Lord your God and walk after other gods and serve them and worship them, I testify against you this day that you shall surely perish.

After you receive the Blessing of the Lord, embrace Him all the more. Double your prayer, worship, bible study, service to Him and praise before Him to insure that His blessing will extend to your future generations.

Chapter Seven
Break Poverty Curses

As the bird by wandering, as the swallow by flying, so the curse causeless shall not come. ***Proverbs 26:2***

In other words, if you are cursed, it is for a reason. I am covering curses here to make sure you have considered every possible reason for poverty in your life. If you are a Christian and you have confessed prosperity, tithed, given offerings and repented of every known sin (such as I had) then there is a good chance that you may have a curse resting upon your life. This is not to say that you are the reason for the curse. You may have inherited a curse when you were born. Curses jump from generation to generation.

Exodus 34:6-7
And the LORD passed by before him, and proclaimed, The LORD, The LORD God, merciful and gracious, longsuffering, and abundant in goodness and truth,

Keeping mercy and loving-kindness for thousands, forgiving iniquity and transgression and sin, but Who will by no means clear the guilty, visiting the iniquity of the fathers upon the children and the children's children, to the third and fourth generation.

Curses always generate from sin; sins someone else in your family, tribe or nation committed. Consider the following verse of scripture:

II Samuel 21:1-3
¹There was a three-year famine in the days of David, year after year; and David inquired of the Lord. The Lord replied, it is on account of Saul and his bloody house, for he put to death the Gibeonites"
²So the king called the Gibeonites now the Gibeonites were not Israelites but of the remnant of the Amorites. The Israelites had sworn to spare them, but Saul in his zeal for the people of Israel and Judah had sought to slay the Gibeonites
³So David said to the Gibeonites, What shall I do for you? How can I make atonement that you may bless the Lord's inheritance?

In **II Samuel 21:1**, the writer describes a famine in land for three full years. Then David inquired of the Lord, and the Lord replied that the famine was because of Saul's bloody house. Once again, David, himself had done nothing, but Saul who was King over the nation of Israel at the time, had committed murder against another tribe of people, the Gibeonites.

In verse 3, David went to the Gibeonites and asked them what is was that he could do to make atonement for the act of Saul. They responded by asking him if seven of Saul's sons be given over to them, that they may hang them to atone for the lives that were taken from them. This request David honored and then the land returned to its rest.

II Samuel 21:14

"And the bones of Saul and Jonathan his son they buried in the country of Benjamin in Zelah in the tomb of Kish, [Saul's] father, and they did all that the king commanded. And after that, God heard and answered when His people prayed for the land.

We see that God responded to the prayers of His people when they atoned for the sin of Saul's house that had been committed.

There are some sinful things in our families that took place in times past that are affecting our lives today. Satan wants to perpetuate the curses to your offspring, especially the curse of poverty. When we investigate the acts and sins of our fathers and forefathers, stand in the gap and repent on behalf of those sins, God will reverse the curse that landed on our lives from generations before.

Deuteronomy 30:1-3

[1]And when all these things have come upon you, the blessings and the curses which I have set before you, and you shall call them to mind among all the nations where the Lord your God has driven you.

[2]And shall return to the Lord your God and obey His voice according to all that I command you today, you and your children, with all your [mind and] heart and with all your being.

[3]Then the Lord your God will restore your fortunes and have compassion upon you and will gather you again from all the nations where He has scattered you.

Thank God that *Galatians 3:13* declares:

[13] Christ purchased our freedom [redeeming us] from the curse (doom) of the Law [and its condemnation] by [Himself] becoming a curse for us, for it is written [in the Scriptures], Cursed is everyone who hangs on a tree (is crucified)

Christ has already destroyed those curses for us. All we have to do is repent, and apply the blood of Jesus to our sins and to the sin of forefathers. We must then move in I'm adopted. I did just a little investigation into my biological background to find that my birth mother was impoverished. I also found this could have been the reason why I was given up for adoption in the first place.

Having been privileged with this information, I knew the spirit of poverty had to be forcefully broken from my life. I had not been the direct cause of the curse's entry, but I believe I inherited it when I was born – a generational curse.

The curse of poverty can also a manifest itself as a mindset. Some of the manifestations of the curse of poverty are: a lack of diligence, the inability to complete things, laziness, a lack of motivation, and taking one step forward and going two steps backward.

A perfect example of a family under a curse of poverty would be the Evans family in the situational comedy "Good Times." No matter how many opportunities to prosper came their way, something would happen and the opportunity would evaporate. If I am correct, they never made it out of the ghetto. This is exactly how the curse of poverty manifests in reality. However, the Evans Family was just like me, always striving to correct the situation, but prosperity always remained out of reach.

I realized that something had to be wrong when I was doing all I could do to walk in prosperity. One of the things I did was to start my own business. My competitors were no more experienced, equipped or well known than I was, but my business just would not take off. Not only did I experience the curse of poverty and defeat in business, but also on my job and it seemed in every area of my life. The world refers to this as "bad luck." Now seemingly, I have entered into a season of prosperity the likes of which I have never experienced before. The breaking of the curse of poverty was the beginning of my breakthrough.

As I previously mentioned in this book, my father was a good man. He was fun-loving, kind and generous. After working for years and financially struggling in production plants, God caused him to be blessed through a mishap at his job.

He built us a beautiful home, gave to the church and afterwards, through the temptation of enemy, fell into secret sin. In 1981 he died suddenly and it was then these things were revealed. Then came the day when all the wealth was gone. The aftermath of my father's premature death left our family in a mountain of unpaid debt. Over a twenty year period our family struggled. There was a period in my life when I was on welfare and receiving food stamps.

It was during this period in 1983 that I became a Christian. I began to practice tithing and my financial situation improved. I was able to secure good jobs, but I was always in survival mode, living paycheck to paycheck. I believed God for prosperity over a period of ten years and nothing happened.

It was not until a few years ago after days of fasting and prayer that the Holy Spirit revealed to me the problem was my father's un-confessed sin. I stood in the gap that day in prayer, confessed my father's sin and asked for forgiveness according to the scripture.

I John 1:9

If we freely admit that we have sinned and confess our sins, He is faithful and just (true to His own nature and promises) and will forgive our sins [dismiss our lawlessness] and [continuously] cleanse us from all unrighteousness [everything not in conformity to His will in purpose, thought, and action].

I asked God to forgive my father for his sins and shortcomings. Then I broke the curse of poverty over our land, our house and our finances. It was not long after this; I received the first $200,000 blessing in our immediate family.

Search your family history. Learn of your family's shortcomings and failures. Stand in the gap and repent for the sins of your fathers, forefathers and then break the curses that resulted. A curse is as a curse does. What do you see that you can't explain? Is it lack, famine, death, sicknesses or mental illness?

If Satan has had you under a curse all of your life, then he is not going to want to let go immediately. Fasting when you pray gives your prayers that extra power. God promises restoration when you repent of your sins and the sins of your forefathers.

Leviticus 26:39-42

[39]And they that are left of you shall pine away in their iniquity in your enemies' lands; and also in the iniquities of their fathers shall they pine away with them.

[40]But if they confess their own and their fathers' iniquity in their treachery which they committed against Me – and also that because they walked contrary to Me

[41]I also walked contrary to them and brought them into the land of their enemies – if then their uncircumcised hearts are humbled and they then accept the punishment for their iniquity,

[42]Then will I [earnestly] remember My covenant with Jacob, My covenant with Isaac, and My covenant with Abraham, and [earnestly] remember the land.

God is, and He will continue to be faithful to honor your prayer of repentance. Your prayer could be like the following:

Father, I come to You today in the Name of Jesus. I ask You to forgive me of my sins and cleanse me of my unrighteousness. I stand in the gap for _____. I ask You to forgive them of the sin of _____ (if you know the sin). I thank You for forgiving them. I ask You to place it under the Blood of Jesus Christ. I break the power of every curse in the name of Jesus. I thank You that every generational curse is broken off my life, my children's life, and family's life in the name of Jesus Christ.

Now begin to pray the blessing over your life according to the following scripture:

Numbers 6:23-26

[23] *"Say to Aaron and his sons, this is the way you shall bless the Israelites. Say to them:"*

[24] *The Lord bless me and watch, guard, and keep me;*

[25] *The Lord make His face to shine upon and enlighten me and be gracious (kind, merciful, and giving favor to me;*

[26] *The Lord lift up His [approving] countenance upon me and give me peace (tranquility of heart and life continually).*

Jesus already broke the curse at Calvary, but it was through prayer and fasting, the revelation of the Holy Spirit and repentance that the curse of poverty was broken from my life. It was then I truly had a chance to walk in the blessings God had for me.

Chapter Eight
Get Into Covenant with God

Covenant is defined by *Webster's New World Dictionary* as a binding or solemn agreement to do a specified thing, and covenant in the Bible also has spiritual ramifications.

We find in Genesis, Chapter 6 the first mention of covenant in the Bible:

Genesis 6:17-18
[17]*"For behold, I, even, I, will bring a flood of waters upon the earth to destroy and make putrid all flesh under the heavens in which are the breath and spirit of life; everything that is on the land shall die."*
[18]*"But I will establish My covenant (promise, pledge) with you, and you shall come into the ark – you and your sons and your wife and your sons' wives with you."*

God establishes His covenant with Noah and he becomes the new father of mankind, virtually replacing Adam. He says further to Noah he and his family will be spared by the flood. God tell Noah He will send a flood to do away with all flesh.

Mankind at that time was totally evil. This was God's way of starting over. He started over by renewing His covenant with someone He saw and determined was righteous.

Genesis 6:5-7:

[5] *"The Lord saw that the wickedness of man was great in the earth, and that every imagination and intention of man on the earth and He was grieved at heart."*

[6] *"So the Lord said, that I will destroy, blot out, and wipe away mankind, whom I have created from the face of the ground-not only man, but the beasts and creeping things and the birds of the air-for it grieves Me and makes Me regretful that I have made them."*

[7] *"But Noah found grace (favor) in the eyes of the Lord."*

Then God vows never again to curse the ground and destroy any living creature by flood anymore. Thus the rainbow is an everlasting sign of God's mercy toward His creation. Noah died 350 years after the Flood that destroyed the earth. He was 950 years old.

God once again began to search for a man with whom He could make covenant. Then in the land of Ur of Chaldees He saw the heart of a man called Abram. Abram's family served false gods. They served gods in the form of statutes, but Abram knew that something was missing.

Abram was like some of us, he knew in his heart the gods his family worshiped could not help him. He sensed in his heart there was another God, the God who sent the rain, sunshine and the harvest. Then God initiated a covenant with Abram.

Genesis 12:1-3

[1] *Now [in Haran} the Lord said to Abram, Go for yourself [for your own advantage] away from your country, from your relatives and your father's house, to the land that I will show you.*

[2]And I will make of you a great nation, and I will bless you [with abundant increase of favors] and make your name famous and distinguished, and you will be a blessing [dispensing good to others].

[3]And I will bless those who bless you [who confer prosperity or happiness upon you] and curse him who curses or uses insolent language toward you; in you will all the families of the earth be blessed [and by you they will bless themselves].

Abram was seventy-five years old when God spoke to him to leave his family. He was obedient and started out in faith, believing God towards a land he had never seen.

This covenant God made with Abram was confirmed and ratified by a blood sacrifice. This was customary with God from the time the Hebrews were in the Wilderness at Sinai.

Genesis 15:9-10; 17-18

[9]And He said to him, Bring to Me a heifer three years old, a she-goat three years old, a ram, three years old, a turtledove and a young pigeon.

[10]And he brought Him all these and cut them down the middle [into halves] and laid each half opposite each other, but the birds, he did not divide.

[17]When the sun had gone down and a [thick] darkness had come on, behold, a smoking oven and a flaming torch passed between those pieces.

[18]On the same day the Lord made a covenant with Abram, saying, To your descendants I have given this land, from the river Euphrates.

God promised Abraham seven things:

(1) I will make of thee a great nation

(2) I will bless thee

(3) I will make thy name great

(4) Thou shall be a blessing

(5) I will bless them that bless thee

(6) I will curse him who curses you

(7) In thee shall the families of the earth be blessed

I outlined this covenant God made with Abraham because this covenant was not annulled, but fulfilled by the birth, ministry, death, burial and resurrection of Jesus Christ 433 years later.

Galatians 3:13-14, 29
[13]Christ purchased our freedom [redeeming us] from the curse (doom) of the Law [and its condemnation] by [Himself} becoming a curse for us, for it is written [in the Scriptures], Cursed is everyone who hangs on a tree (is crucified);
[14]To the end that through [their receiving] Christ Jesus, the blessing [promised] to Abraham might come upon the Gentiles, so that we through faith might [all] receive [the realization of] the promise of the [Holy] Spirit.
[29]And if you belong to Christ [are in Him Who is Abraham's Seed], then you are Abraham's Offspring and [spiritual] heirs according to the promise.

Until I realized I was a spiritual heir of Abraham, I used to be so envious of the Jewish nation. They are two percent of the population of the earth, but they have ninety percent of all the wealth in the world! Then God revealed to me that I was a Jew as well!

This meant the same Abrahamic blessing could be upon my life too! Before you commit me to the funny farm, read the following scripture:

Romans 2:28-29

28For he is not a [real] Jew who is only one outwardly and publicly, nor is true] circumcision something external and physical,

29But he is a Jew who is one inwardly, and [true] circumcision is of the heart, a spiritual and not a literal [manner]. His praise is not from men but from God.

Amen! We are spiritual Jews and entitled to the covenant that God made with Abraham, not just the spiritual blessing of righteousness by faith, but also material wealth.

Jesus finalized this covenant through His death on the Cross. Before He was to die, He instituted the Last Supper so we would remember He sacrificed Himself, pouring out His own blood. The Covenant God made with Abraham in the Old Covenant is fulfilled by the death and resurrection of Jesus Christ in the New Covenant. This is why He said to remember Him with the bread and the wine.

I Corinthians 11:23-24

And when He had given thanks, He broke [it] and said, Take, eat, This is My body, which is broken for you. Do this to call Me [affectionately] to remembrance.

Similarly, when supper was ended, He took the cup also, saying, This cup is the new covenant [ratified and established] in My blood. Do this as often as you drink [it], to call Me [affectionately] to remembrance.

45

By faith, I continually partake of communion in order to honor what Jesus did for me on the Cross. In this way I constantly remember and show my appreciation for the covenant that we have with God because of His sacrifice. The Bible refers to the communion cup as the "cup of blessing" in *I Corinthians 10:16*:

The cup of blessing [of wine at the Lord's Supper] upon which we ask [God's] blessing, does it not mean [that in drinking it] we participate in and share a fellowship (a communion) in the blood of Christ (the Messiah)? The bread which we break, does it not mean [that in eating it] we participate in and share a fellowship (a communion) in the body of Christ?

When you partake of the elements of communion, the bread and the wine, you confirm to yourself, all of heaven, all of hell that you are in covenant with Almighty God. You establish yourself in the Covenant of God, so that the Covenant of God can be established in you. You establish yourself in peace, righteousness, healing and wealth.

The Hebrew word for this most blessed condition is "shalom." It means nothing missing, nothing broken. One of God's redemptive names is Jehovah-Shalom. His very name means peace. When you have everything you need, are protected from danger, bills are paid, you and your family are well and you are in covenant with God, the end result will be peace.

I love to do Sunday afternoon evangelism. I will pull the phone book out and just start calling people over the phone. I sometimes call those listed in the phonebook who live in the most affluent neighborhoods in our state. When I ask them if I can pray for them, a lot of them respond "no," we don't have need for anything." It is then that I ask them can I pray for their protection going up and down the highway.

My goal is to make them think about what they are saying, prompt them to humble themselves and admit that their wealth can't cover every aspect of their lives. Only a covenant with God can do that. My brother, my sister get into covenant with God, pray this prayer:

Dear Heavenly Father:

Today I renew my covenant with You. I receive Your covering and the envelopment of Your amazing grace. I am forgetting all the hindrances and the weights of my past. I thank You that I am empowered to press towards the mark of the high calling in Christ Jesus.

I am putting on the mind of Christ. I am letting You have Your full being in me. I am keeping my mind stayed on You and your Holy Word. I am reminding myself You will keep me and keep me in perfect peace because my mind is stayed on Thee.

I covenant with You, that I will commit my financial life to You. I receive my inheritance because I am the Seed of Abraham. I am blessed because he was blessed. I receive You as Jehovah Jireh, my Provider and as the Lord of the Harvest, In Jesus Name, Amen.

Chapter Nine
Sow Into Your Financial Harvest

Genesis 1:11
"And God said, Let the earth put forth [tender] vegetation: plants yielding seed and fruit trees yielding fruit whose seed is in itself, each according to its kind, upon the earth. And it was so.

Sowing and reaping is nothing new. God instituted this spiritual law at the beginning of creation. It is an everlasting principle that will not fade away. Jesus further expounded on this law and how it affects our finances as Christians in the New Testament:

Luke 6:38
"Give, and gifts will be given to you; good measure, pressed down, shaken together, and running over, will they pour into [the pouch formed by the bosom of your robe and used as a bag]. For [with the measure you use when you confer benefits on others], it will be measured back to you."

Jesus, Himself, is telling us you cannot lose by giving. You can only create a financial harvest. Just as in the natural every seed produces after its own kind, so it is in the spiritual realm.

If you sow clothes, you will reap clothes. If you sow kindness, you will reap kindness; if you sow mercy, you will reap mercy and if you sow money, you will reap money. Everything will reproduce after the kind of seed sown. I understand you have probably heard this a lot before now. Sometimes this scripture promise is met with much skepticism, but Jesus said it, so it has to be true.

The Tithe

The foundation of your giving should first of all be the tithe, which God calls holy unto Him.

Malachi 3:8-9
[8] "Will a man rob or defraud God? Yet you rob and defraud Me. But you say, In what way do we rob and defraud You? [You have withheld your] tithes and offerings.
[9] "You are cursed with the curse, for you are robbing Me, even this whole nation."

Just as you have everything to gain by giving, you have everything to lose by not tithing. Tithing on everything that you earn is God's command and your security blanket for receiving your financial harvest. The end of all God's commands is blessing. He knows what it takes for you to be truly blessed. However, God has a test that you must pass if you really want a financial harvest.

Proverbs 3:9-10
[9] "Honor the Lord with your capital and sufficiency [from righteous labors] and with the firstfruits of all your income."
[10] "So shall your storage places be filled with plenty, and your vats shall be overflowing with new wine."

Our spiritual father, Abraham, whom I discussed in the previous chapter, was a dedicated tither.

Hebrews 7:1, 2

[1] "For this Melchizedek, King of Salem [and] priest of the Most high God, met Abraham as he returned from the slaughter of the kings and blessed him.

[2] And Abraham gave to him a tenth portion of all [the spoil]. He is primarily, as his name when translated indicates, king of righteousness, and the he is also king of Salem, which means king of peace."

Melchizedek is considered to be a Theopany, an Old Testament appearance of Christ, or a type of Christ. He was the King-Priest of Salem. After Abraham's return from the defeat and slaying of Chedorlamer, along with the King of Sodom, Abraham went to Melchizedek and gave him a tenth of the spoil. As we will examine in the next few paragraphs in the Old Testament, when someone wanted to tithe, they took their portion to the high priest.

The King of Sodom tried to convince Abraham to keep what remained for himself, but Abraham rebuked him to his face. Essentially, Abraham was saying to the King of Sodom God would bless him without his contributions to his finances. After Abraham was obedient to tithe to Melchizedek, God appeared to Abraham and confirmed His blessing on his life.

Genesis 14:21-23

[21]*"And the King of Sodom said to Abram, give me the persons and keep the goods for yourself.*

[22]*But Abram said to the king of Sodom, I have lifted up my hand and sworn to the Lord, God Most High, The Possessor and Maker of heaven and earth,*

[23]*That I would not take a thread or a shoelace or anything that is yours, lest you should say, I have made Abram rich."*

Genesis 15:1

After these things, the word of the Lord came to Abram in a vision, saying, Fear not, Abram, I am your Shield, your abundant compensation, and your reward shall be exceedingly great."

So tithing is a sacred sacrifice unto God. The tithe is a monetary representation your life. We spend many hours away from home trying to earn a living. The money we earn is precious and God knows that it is precious to us. This is why the tithe is holy to God and a sweet-smelling sacrifice in His nostrils. So it is important not to treat the tithe lightly. In **Deuteronomy 26:1-9** the details of how the tithe was to be presented to the High Priest are written:

[1]*"When you have come into the land which the Lord your God gives you as an inheritance and possess it and live in it,*

[2]*You shall take some the first of all the produce of the soil which you harvest form the land the Lord your God gives you and put in a basket, and go to the place [the sanctuary] which the Lord your God has chosen as the abiding place for His Name [and His presence].*

³And you shall go the priest who is in office in those days, and say to him, I give thanks this day to the Lord your God that I have come to the land which the Lord swore to our fathers to give us.

⁴And the priest shall say before the Lord your god, a wandering and lost Aramean ready to perish was my father, and he went down into Egypt and sojourned there, few in number, and he became there a nation, great, mighty, and numerous.

⁵And the Egyptians treated us very badly and afflicted us and laid upon us hard labor.

⁶And when we cried to the Lord, the God of our fathers, the Lord heard our voice and looked on our affliction and our labor and our [cruel] oppression;

⁷And the Lord brought us forth out of Egypt with a mighty hand and with an outstretched arm, and with great (awesome) power and with signs and wonders;

⁸And He brought us into this place and gave us this land, a land flowing with milk and honey.

⁹And now, behold, I bring the firstfruits of the ground which You, O Lord, have given me. And you shall set it down before the Lord your God and worship before the Lord your God."

We are to take the tithe to the high priest of our day: before the Pastor, into the Church where the presence of God dwells. Give your tithe in a place where people are being saved, set free from bondages and delivered. Give your tithe in a place where people are being taught the infilling of the Holy Spirit, people are ministered to by benevolence; divine healing and the message that God wants to bless you, or, in other words, the full Gospel.

I know that everyone reading this book will not agree with me, but the presence of God does not dwell in every church. It does no good to plant seed in unfertile ground and I consider it sin for me to plant God's holy tithe in a place where His Spirit does not dwell. Seek the Lord and He will direct you where to offer your tithe. So the conclusion to all that I have said is tithing is basic and essential to receiving your financial harvest.

I know of a family in the five-fold ministry in the Body of Christ. They are wonderful people and they are anointed people. However, they are broke people, having always struggled financially.

I often wondered why they moved from house to house, why they drove older vehicles and never seemed to have enough money. I foolishly thought that they stayed under attack from the devil because they were so anointed. Then one day while visiting them, the father in the family told me that he did not believe in tithing. He said tithing was the old law and bondage. Suddenly I knew why they had suffered financially and had no stability. They were robbing God and they were cursed with curse.

Jesus said in *Matthew 5:17-19*:

[17] *"Do not think that I have come to do away with or undo the Law or the Prophets; I have come not to do away with or undo but to complete and fulfill them.*

[18] *For truly I tell you, until the sky and earth pass away and perish, not one smallest letter nor one little hook [identifying certain Hebrew letters] will pass from the Law until all things [it foreshadows] are accomplished.*

19Whoever then breaks or does away with or relaxes one the least [important] of these commandments and teaches men so shall be called least [important] in the kingdom of heaven, but he who practices them and teaches other to do so shall be called great in the kingdom of heaven.."

Jesus is saying here just because it's written in the Old Testament Law and the Books of the Prophets do not mean it's not important. He does not invalidate what was written or spoken before His coming, but He is the fulfillment and the end of it. So even though tithing is in the Old Testament, it is still the New Testament thing to do.

If you refuse to tithe, following the commandment of God, then forget about receiving a financial harvest from Him. I remember thinking to myself, why take the chance, do it anyway just because God said it. Do it because you love Him and want to worship Him with the things that are important to you.

The Ten Commandments were established for us in the Old Testament, but yet we as 21st Century Christians need to obey them or still suffer the consequences. Again, God's commandments are always for our benefit. Tithing is for our benefit. Look at the promise for the person who tithes set forth in *Malachi 3:10-12*:

10"Bring all the tithes (the whole tenth of your income) into the storehouse, that there may be food in My house, and prove Me not by it, says the Lord of hosts, if I will not open the windows of heaven and pour you out a blessing, that there shall not be room enough to receive it.

[11]"And I will rebuke the devourer [insects and plagues] for your sakes and he shall not destroy the fruits of your ground, neither shall your vine drop its fruit before the time in the field, says the Lord of hosts."
[12]"And all nations shall call you happy and blessed, for you shall be a land of delight, says the Lord of hosts."

Tithing is the very least one should do if you are believing God for a supernatural financial harvest. God simply asks that we sacrifice ten percent of our earnings for the work of the church body. In return He has promised to open the windows of heaven and pour us out a blessing. That is an excellent rate of exchange!

One Sunday morning, I had stopped at a gas station to get a newspaper for my mother. As I walked into the gas station, an elderly woman was sitting in what appeared to be a very beaten up car. She looked as if she was dressed for church. I asked her if she needed help and she said she just thought she needed some oil in her car. I said "okay" and I continued on down the street. I told the Lord, "Lord, I would buy that lady a car if I had the money." The Holy Spirit said to me, "You do have the money." This is sort of silly to admit, but I said to the Lord, "I do have the money, don't I?"

Sometimes when you have experienced lack for so long, you can forget you have the resources available to help someone else. I told the Lord I thought the lady was going to think I was crazy when I offered to buy her a car, but I was obedient.

When I arrived back at the gas station, she was still there, now with the hood up. I asked her again could I help her. She said the car had just died on her. I told her, "Lady, the Lord has told me to buy you a car." She looked so astonished, as I expected she would and I asked her for her address. I told her I would get back in touch with her when I had found the car.

Over the next ten days or so, I kicked myself for saying that, but God reiterated to me I had promised to buy her a car. In the Book of James it talks about people praying for others with needs, but not lifting a finger to meet the need.

Some tithe their net, but my faith soared when I began to tithe on the gross amount I earned. This truly was a sacrifice for me. My obedience to paying the tithe made me feel secure because I knew I was obeying God and He would take care of me. I never lacked anything for long, something would always happen to cause my needs to be met. Paying my tithes was the best investment that I could make towards the prosperity of my life!

Giving to the Poor

An additional mode of giving is giving to the poor. *Proverbs 14:31* says:

"He who oppresses the poor reproaches, mocks, and insults his Maker, but he who is kind and merciful to the needy honors Him."

Matthew 6:2-4 says:

[2] *"Thus, whenever you give to the poor; do not blow a trumpet before you, as the hypocrites in the synagogues and in the streets like to do, that they may be recognized and honored and praised by men."*
[3] *"Truly I tell you, they have their reward in full already.*
[4] *But when you give to charity, do not let your left hand know what your right hand is doing, so that you deeds of*

charity may be in secret; and your Father Who sees in secret will reward you openly."

First, the Word shows us it is God's will we give to the poor and the subsequent verses reveal there is a reward when we give to the poor in secret.

I met a young lady one day at the post office in my town. We began to talk and I discovered that she had five children. I knew that this was a potential giving opportunity, so I gave her my number.

It was about a month later that she called. She said that her baby needed pampers and that she did not have any money. At this time I was living paycheck to paycheck myself and had little money at the time of this phone call. I sensed the desperation in her voice and I told her that I would get them.

I remember going to the dollar store and purchasing the biggest package of pampers they had for about $10.00. When I gave them to her she was so grateful.

This was just a few days after I had attended church and had given my tithes as well. A couple of days later, I had a check in my hands for approximately $1,000.00. I remember saying to myself this really works! I had compounded two forms of giving that week and received a glorious harvest! This was one of the things that turned me on to giving to the poor in addition to my tithes and offerings.

James 2:15-16
¹⁵If a brother or sister is poorly clad and lack food for each day,

¹⁶And one of you say to him, Good-bye! Keep [yourself] warm and well fed, without giving him the necessities for the body, what good does that do?

I had the money to meet her need. I had never given a car away before, but I was believing God for an even bigger harvest.

When we give to the poor and needy, we are lending to the Lord and He will repay what we have given. I believed for a harvest I had never received before, so I had to sow a seed I had never sown before.

I began to look around for a car for her. I figured I would spend about a small amount for a car for someone else. I checked a couple of the used car lots. But then I explained my concerns to the Lord about spending so much, even though I wanted to be obedient. I knew that giving her another clunker was simply out of the question.

One evening I went to a leadership banquet and one of my neighbors who was there, told me that he was selling his Volvo. I had seen the Volvo and it looked pretty good and I knew that he kept it in excellent condition. He asked me if I wanted to test drive it for a day. I drove the car to work the next day and I fell in love with it. I wanted the car for myself. My son then drove the car and he fell in love with the car too. I found myself in a dilemma. How was I going to buy this car, and give the car to the lady with the broken vehicle?

I wrestled for about a week. I did not want to give the car up, neither did my son. Finally, I got up and sat on the edge of the bed. I know that it was the voice of the Holy Spirit talking to me which said, "Why don't you sow the car and believe Me for your dream car?"

I knew deep in the heart that this was the right thing to do. It made perfect sense to me. I called my son in and I told him what the Lord had revealed to me. We prayed a prayer of agreement to commit this car as a seed for all our future cars.

I felt the greatest sense of peace afterwards. I knew that I was doing the perfect will of God, for myself and for that lady. When I took the car to her, she could not believe that someone was buying her a car. She said she had never experienced anything like this before. She was overwhelmed. I handed the title to her, blessed her, told her to praise Jesus and said good-bye. This was a very nice car, nothing beat up, scratched up or unsightly. This was the best that I could give her.

The Father gave His best to us when He gave Jesus so He might receive many sons:

John 3:16
"For God so greatly loved and dearly prized the world that He [even] gave up His only begotten [unique] Son, so that whoever believes in Him shall not perish, but have eternal life."

I did not give out of my abundance, believe me, I had to sacrifice to buy that car. But consider what *II Corinthians 9:6* says:

"[Remember] this: he who sows sparingly and grudgingly will also reap sparingly and grudgingly, and he who sows generously [that blessings may come to someone] will also reap generously and with blessings."

I was excited. I had just put myself in a position to receive from the Lord of the Harvest!

Milton Hershey, The Epitome of Giving

Most of us have eaten a Hershey bar sometime during our lifetime. It was not until recently I discovered what a generous man Milton Hershey proved to be. His home for orphans inherited the eight hundred million dollar fortune of Milton Hershey.

Who was this Milton Hershey? He was a poor child from Hockersville, Pennsylvania. His religious background was established from his family's attendance at a Mennonite Church.

When Milton Hershey finally came into his fortune and needed a factory to produce his candies, he built an entire city to accommodate it. It was also at this time he initiated and completed the Milton Hershey School. Milton Hershey and his wife were childless. He and his wife wanted to give those children everything he, Milton Hershey, did not have as a child and he made sure they were taught and understood the scriptures.

It is also said during the great depression, Milton Hershey and all of his ventures prospered. Milton Hershey believed in giving to the poor. He gave a whole town the very best his wealth could provide for them. The Milton Hershey School, the town of Hershey, Pennsylvania and his company, Hershey Foods are all a testament to God's faithfulness to His Word and to Milton Hershey, a man who considered the poor.

Psalms 41:1
Blessed (happy, fortunate, to be envied) is he who considers the weak and the poor; the Lord will deliver him in the time of evil and trouble.

Investing in the Gospel

III John 5-8
[5]Beloved, it is a fine and faithful work that you are doing when you give any service to the [Christian] brethren, and [especially when they are] strangers.

[6]They have testified before the church of your love and friendship. You will do well to forward them on their journey [and you will please do so] in a way worthy of God's [service].

[7]For these traveling missionaries have gone out for the Name's sake (for His sake) and are accepting nothing from the Gentiles (the heathen).

[8]So we ourselves ought to support such people {to welcome and provide for them], in order that we may be fellow workers in the Truth (the whole Gospel) and co-operate with its teachers.

These scriptures tell us that it is good to sow into the ministry of missionaries. That is giving hospitality and financial assistance for traveling missionaries who teach true Christian doctrine.

When you sow into a person or organization that is bringing the Gospel, the scripture declares that you are a fellow worker with that person or group and you share in the fruits of their labor among the lost.

There are missionaries who are in full-time ministry, preaching all over the world. They are not hard to find.

I am sure that there is a mission near you, a soup kitchen feeding the hungry, a ministry providing clothing, a ministry to the sick and "shut-in". All these are ways of investing in the spreading of the Gospel to others. Providing food and shelter for these missionaries is also a way to invest in the Gospel.

Sowing in Famine

Isaac sowed during a famine at Gerar and received one hundred fold.

Genesis 26:1, 12
[1]And there was a famine in the land, other than the former famine that was in the days of Abraham. And Isaac went to Gerar, to Abimelech king of the Philistines.
[12]Then Isaac sowed seed in that land and received in the same year a hundred times as much as he had planted and the Lord favored him with blessings.

Times of famine represent scarcity. If you listen to reason, a famine would not be the right time to sow seed, if you expect to get a harvest. But Isaac obeyed God Who always goes against the grain and he received much more favor and blessings from the Lord.

Before you get to your wealthy place, there will be seasons of famine in your land that will require you to sow seed. This is the time to sow seed.

Not only is it the time to sow, but it is an excellent opportunity to prove your commitment and faithfulness to God in the area of finance. God is looking for people to bless so that they can become a blessing. But He looks to see if you will obey Him in faith when it looks like there is no way you will get a return on your seed sown. He needs to know that He can trust you.

Luke 16:10-12

10 He who is faithful in a very little [thing] is faithful also in much, and he who is dishonest and unjust in a very little [thing] is dishonest and unjust also in much.

11 Therefore if you have not been faithful in the [case of] unrighteous mammon (deceitful riches, money, possessions), who will entrust to you the true riches?

12 And if you have not proved faithful in that which belongs to another [whether God or man], who will give you that which is your own [that is, the true riches]?

"A Generous Spirit May Yield a Generous Life Span"

No matter what form of giving that you choose to sow into your financial harvest, consider the following article from the November 16th, 2002 issue of USA today:

Older adults who live by the adage: "It's more blessed to give than to receive" could enjoy longer life spans than people still focused on "gimme" in later years, suggests a pioneering new study.

"It's the first one to compare how giving and receiving in daily life affect longevity, and researchers say the findings are surprising. Scientists have long known that social contact improves health and promotes longer life."

"Our results strongly suggest that giving makes a difference in terms of health," says psychologist Stephanie Brown of the university's Institute for Social Research."

Isn't remarkable that even the world is beginning to learn that it is more blessed to give than to receive? Truly what God declares to us in His word is for our good and for His glory.

CHAPTER TEN
Meditate on the Word of God

Joshua 1:8

"This Book of the Law shall not depart out of your mouth, but you shall meditate on it day and night, that you may observe and do according to all that is written in it. For then you will make your way prosperous, and then you shall deal wisely and have good success."

The Webster's New World Dictionary defines the word "meditation" as reflecting upon; pondering; to thinking deeply and continuously. The Hebrew meaning for this word "meditate" is to mutter, to speak to one's self. Is it not a wonder that God told Joshua to meditate on the Word. When you are meditating on the Word of God, not only are you thinking and reflecting upon it, but sometimes you may find yourself repeating what it has to say with your lips.

Joshua inherited the leadership responsibility that was passed to Him from God after Moses' death. I wonder why God didn't tell Joshua to pray four hours a day, or to fast three days a month. No, God told Joshua to meditate upon His word. God's Word is true. It is safe to focus on what the Word of God says.

We meditate on something every day. It might be the financial news coming from the broadcasts of CNN. It may be advice from your financial advisor. What about the stock market reports in these financially rocky times?

Meditating on the promises of God will cause you to focus on the solution, instead of the needs and financial lack you may be experiencing. Consider ***Philippians 4:4***:

For the rest, brethren, whatever is true, whatever is worthy of reverence and is honorable and seemly, whatever is just, whatever is pure, whatever is lovely and lovable, whatever is kind and winsome and gracious, if there is any virtue and excellence, if there is anything worthy of praise, think on and weigh and take account of these things [fix your minds on them].

My late Bishop, George D. Lee III, always told us: "you will always gravitate or take action towards your most dominate thought." If you meditate on poverty, you will subconsciously take steps to insure you experience poverty. If you meditate on prosperity, you will take actions that will result in prosperity.

Proverbs 23:7 declares: "*As a man thinks in his heart, so is he.*"

God gave us our imaginations to aide in meditation. The devil longs to pervert the imagination with negativity, perverse things and with false events appearing real, which is the essence of FEAR.

The best way to eliminate the negative, which is all around us, is to meditate on the promises of God. As stated in ***II Corinthians 1:20***, "*For as many are the promises of God, they all find their Yes [answer] in Him*

[Christ]. For this reason we utter the Amen (so be it) to God through Him [in His Person and by His agency] to the glory of God."

The Bible declares that all His promises are yes! So why not meditate on what He says is yours by inheritance. No matter what is going on around you, as you meditate on Truth, faith will come and peace will come.

I use my imagination as a tool to motivate me to pray when I don't feel like it, to make confessions when I don't feel like it and to give thanks to God when I don't feel like it.

I paste pictures that represent the life that I want to live on my prayer room walls that constantly invade my imagination when I am in that place of prayer. My imagination generates my thoughts, and thoughts lead to action and actions bring forth fruit.

God told Abraham to meditate on the stars of the sky because this would be representation of his posterity. Every time he looked into the heavens, even though he was childless, he had a visual image of countless sons and daughters that would come from his loins and his spiritual heritage. Begin to meditate on prosperity!

Chapter Eleven
Create Wealth with the Spoken Word

Mark 11:23-24
[23] "Truly I tell you, whoever says to this mountain, Be lifted up and thrown into the sea! And does not doubt at all in his heart but believes that what he says will take place, it will be done for him."
[24] "For this reason I am telling you, whatever you ask for in prayer, believe (trust and be confident) that it is granted to you, and you will [get it]."

This is a wonderful promise from the Word of God. I did not see the manifestation of my financial harvest until I began to confess what the Word of God says regarding my finances. It's kind of funny the way I actually started. I began confessing the Word of God around the time when everyone was concerned about Y2K. This was in 1999 and just before the turning of the year 2000. Everyone was telling me all the computers were going to go haywire. I began to think it would be great perhaps to have all my debt cancelled by this phenomenon.

Of course, at first I was joking with myself, but then I began to seriously think about how nice it would be to have all my debts supernaturally cancelled. I told myself I would begin to create it through my confessions. I believed that my mouth had power. Mark 11:23 was clear about this and I wanted to see what would happen. God wants His people to stop saying what they have, and to start having what they say.

It could not do any further damage to my credit or financial circumstances. I was already in the worst financial shape that I could be already. I saw this as a chance for a breakthrough and an opportunity to experience and learn more about the faithfulness of God's Word.

I began to confess in November of 1999, "Lord, I thank you that on January 1st, the year 2000, my car and all my debts will be paid off." At first, my mouth was confessing it, but my heart had not caught up with what my mouth had to say. In other words, I did not pay any attention to my head. I just kept on confessing that I would be debt-free on January 1^{st,} the year 2000.

I actually came to believe with my heart and head that God was going to supernaturally wipe out all my debt in those computers. I had a knowing in my heart that I could not explain. I don't know if I was spiritually right or wrong, but I knew that supernatural debt cancellation was in the Bible.

II Kings 4:1-7

[1]*Now the wife of a son of the prophets cried to Elisha, Your servant my husband is head, and you know that your servant feared the Lord. But the creditor has come to take my two sons to be his slaves.*

[2]*Elisha said to her, What shall I do for you? Tell me, what have you [of sale value] in the house? She said, Your handmaid has nothing in the house except a jar of oil.*

[3]*Then he said, Go around and borrow vessels from all your neighbors, empty vessels-and not a few.*

[4]*And when you come in, shut the door upon you and your sons. Then pour out [the oil you have] into all those vessels, setting aside each one when it is full.*

[5]*So she went from him and shut the door upon herself and her sons, who brought to there the vessels as she poured the oil.*

[6]*When the vessels were all full, she said to her son, Bring me another vessel. And he said to her, There is not a one left. Then the oil stopped multiplying.*

[7]*Then she came and told the man of God. He said Go, sell the oil and pay your debt, and you and your sons live on the rest.*

Enslavement for debt was the practice in Israel at the time in which Elisha ministers to this woman. It was a common practice. The scripture says that this woman was the wife of one of the sons of prophets. For whatever reason, she was deeply in debt and the bill collectors were coming to apprehend two of her sons to make slaves of them.

Of course, the advice Elisha gave her did not make any sense. To take an empty vessel, take the oil you have, and pour it into all the other vessels you collect? She apparently was a woman of faith because she obeyed the prophet of God.

The whole point is writing this book is to tell you that you don't need rich relatives, a friendship the President of the bank on the corner or A-1 credit to create wealth. All you need is the Word of God. God can bless you when you have nothing. As a matter of fact, He does His best work when you have nothing because then He gets the glory! Our part is to research to see what the Word of God has to say, believe and act on it, speak it out of our mouths and then having done all, stand on it.

We have the same creative ability as God because we were created in His image. Okay, you might be saying "now, you have just spoiled everything that you have said before." Once again consider what the Word of God says about you, mankind, His creation:

Genesis 1:1-3, 26
[1]In the beginning God (prepared, formed, fashioned, and) created the heavens and the earth.
[2]The earth was without form and an empty waste, and darkness was upon the face of the very great deep. The [3]Spirit of God was moving (hovering, brooding) over the face of the waters.
[26]God said, Let Us [Father, Son, and Holy Spirit] make mankind in Our image, after Our likeness, and let them have complete authority over the fish of the sea, the birds of the air, the [tame] beasts, and over all the earth, and over everything that creeps upon the earth.

It is clear in Genesis Chapter 1, everything God created, except man; He created it by the words that came from His mouth. God then declares that man will have dominion over the earth also. Man has dominion by the words that come from his mouth. Jesus said in *Matthew 12:37*:

"For by your words you will be justified and acquitted, and by your words you will be condemned and acquitted."

Notice it is by your words things happen, not by God's words. So God has given us His creative ability. When you combine your creative ability with the Word of God, prosperity, healing, deliverance and whatever else you need will be the result!

As I continually confessed and thanked God my debts were canceled on January 1st, 2000, expectation and excitement began to build in my spirit as I headed towards the New Year. January 1st rolled around and there were no major Y2K problems anywhere. I was somewhat disappointed, but not discouraged. I continued to confess and praise God my car and debts were paid off in Jesus Name.

Then on January 11, 2000, something happened. This particular morning I overslept. I did not get to spend the kind of quality time I like with the Lord before I left for work. I kept on hearing the Holy Spirit say "pray, pray, pray." So I was obedient. As soon as I was on my face before the Lord, the presence of the Holy Spirit came upon me. I was in an intercessory mode and kept asking the Lord for His mercy and His protection with many tears.

When I got up from prayer to go to work, I kept on thinking to myself "what was that all about?" I work approximately ten miles from my job, and about half way there, crossing a major bridge, I looked in front of me to see a tractor trailer truck heading straight for me. The bridge was situated high off the ground in the 500 to 600 feet. I hit the end of the bridge in order to miss the truck hitting me head on. My car, headed off the embankment, hit a telephone company utility pole (and I believe some angels) just kept me from going over. My air bags had deployed. The truck barely missed me, but I was safe.

I was stunned as I walked away from my car. Now I knew what and why the Holy Spirit was encouraging me to pray before I left home. This was a prayer that saved my life. The funny thing was the only thing injured was my left pinky finger. It had a nasty fracture, other than that I was fine.

I know that you are probably saying "I don't want money that badly, can't I get it some other way?" My answer is yes, but this is how God initially brought wealth to me. He brought the opportunity to me in spite of my ignorance of what I was saying and what it would actually mean. Since then I have gained more wisdom and I have learned to be very specific in my confessions. He is God and your Father, He can get your wealth to you in any way He desires, but He cannot and will not rain money on you out of the sky. It has to come from somewhere in the monetary system!

He used this accident to get a two-hundred thousand dollar settlement into my hands and the only thing that I suffered was a broken finger. Most of us think of God blessing us with a bag of money dropped at our door, out of nowhere. I am sure that God can rain money out of heaven if He wanted too, He's God. He is God Almighty, Possessor and Creator of Heaven and Earth! He can do anything and everything that we are willing to believe Him for. Our job is to not limit God! He is Jehovah Jireh!

I believe this accident was directly related to what I had been previously confessing with my mouth. Did it happen exactly on January 1, 2000? No, but it did occur ten days after the original date I had confessed. The accident put me in position to pay off my car and all my other debts just like I had been saying.

About a month after the accident, the insurance company paid off my car. Praise the Lord! It's true, confession brings possession!

Did you know that Jesus watches over your words to perform them? Another translation says "He is the High Priest of our confession."

Hebrews 3:1
Wherefore, holy brethren, partakers of the heavenly calling, consider the Apostle and High Priest of our profession, Christ Jesus;

The word "profession" is translated "confession" from its Greek origins. Either way, Jesus, Himself, is listening and is faithful to bring what you say to pass. He is also merciful because He knows the words you say in folly. Words like:

I could have died laughing.

She killed me by doing when she spoke.

I'd die if I got caught doing that.

The angels are also listening and acting on your words. **Psalms 103:20** says,

"Bless (affectionately, gratefully praise) the Lord, you His angels, you mighty ones who do His commandments, hearkening to the voice of His word."

Lastly, **Proverbs 18:20-21** proclaims:

[20]*A man's self shall be filled with the fruit of his mouth; and with the consequence of his words he must be satisfied [whether good or evil].*

[21]*"Death and life are in the power of the tongue, and they who indulge in it shall eat the fruit of it [for death or life].*

God has given our tongue to us for more than the tasting of delicious foods. He has given the tongue to those of us who have nothing, so that we can take His word and create wealth!

CHAPTER TWELVE
Give God Praise in Advance

Habakkuk 3:18
Though the fig tree does not blossom and there is no fruit on the vines, [though] the product of the olive fails and the fields yield no food, though the flock is cut off from the fold and there is no cattle in the stalls, yet I will rejoice in the Lord: I will exult in the [victorious] God of my salvation!

As I began to believe the Lord for a financial harvest, I determined in my heart I was going to praise Him, whether I saw anything or not. One thing that Satan knows is that you become a dangerous man or woman when you start to sow into the Kingdom of God. He knows it is only a matter of time before you receive a harvest. You become more dangerous to Satan when you praise God. Praise stills enemy and shuts him down. Praise refocuses your attention on God, instead of your circumstances.

There will be times after you have done all, and are standing, you will have to praise God in spite of what you see. Satan, your adversary, will be right there to tell you God's Word will not produce your financial harvest. He will try to get you to accept the circumstances around you and give up. This is when you must do what the Prophet Habakkuk did. You must praise God when it looks as if you will always have lack, and when it appears your harvest is not coming in.

This kind of sacrificial praise actually waters the financial seeds you have sown. Praise is a spiritual weapon that will whip the devil every time. He knows this and will try to bombard you with doubt and unbelief, which can lead to depression and stop your praise!

Paul and Silas had done nothing wrong. They were put in prison for preaching the Gospel of Jesus Christ! Look at what happened to them in prison when they began to praise God in the midst of very unpleasant circumstances:

Acts 16:23-26
23 And when they had struck them with many blows, they threw them into prison, charging the jailer to keep them safely.
24 He, having received [so strict a] charge, put them into the inner prison (the dungeon) and fastened their feet in the stocks,
25 But about midnight, as Paul and Silas were praying and singing hymns of praise to God, and the [other] prisoners were listening to them."
26 Suddenly there was a great earthquake, so that the very foundations of the prison were shaken; and at once all

the doors were opened and everyone's shackles were unfastened.

I am sure as those prisoners listened to Paul and Silas praising God, they said to themselves and to each other, what do they have to sing about? They were in a rat infested, dirty damp prison basement.

It takes real faith to lift up your hands and praise God, or give Him a praise offering in the dance when you are suffering lack, poverty and financial shortages. Yet God will honor the sacrificial praise you give Him before you see your promised land.

CHAPTER THIRTEEN
Loose the Harvest

Daniel 10:12-13
[12]Then he said to me, Fear not, Daniel, for from the first day that you set your mind and heart to understand and to humble yourself before your God, you words were heard, and I have come as a consequence of [and in response to] your words.
[13]But the prince of the kingdom of Persia withstood me for twenty-one days. Then Michael, one of the chief [of the celestial] princes, came to help me, for I remained there with the kings of Persia.

Daniel, God's greatly beloved, began to fast and pray in order to receive revelation from the Lord. We see by this passage of scripture the messenger angel, Gabriel, told Daniel his prayer had been answered from the first day he set his heart to seek God. The prince of Persia in this passage of scripture is well known to refer to the devil, or the prince of darkness.

After you have completed all the other steps, it will be absolutely necessary for you to do spiritual warfare over your harvest. Your prayers and your words can either aid or lend defeat to the angels at harvest time. The devil does want you to be blessed and endeavors to delay your harvest beyond God's appointed time.

I remember on this occasion my harvest had manifested in the natural and all there was left to do was to receive my check in the mail. It seemed it took forever to receive that check. Then the Lord instructed me to use the principles of binding and loosing to move my harvest into my hands. If the enemy can't stop your financial harvest, he will try to delay it actually getting into your hands with red tape by those handling it.

Matthew 18:18
Truly I tell you, whatever you forbid and declare to be improper and unlawful on earth must be what is already forbidden in heaven, and whatever you permit and declare proper and lawful on earth must be what is already permitted in heaven.

Poverty and lack are forbidden in heaven. Wealth is lawful and necessary for your life on the earth so that God can use you to establish His covenant. The Lord also revealed the devil had called on reinforcements to delay my harvest and I was to call others to reinforce my prayers of binding and loosing.

We all fasted and prayed for about a day, binding the devil and loosing this harvest. That very afternoon I received a phone call from my lawyer announcing I would be receiving a very large check the next day.

So what is it you must do to loose the harvest?

I prayed the following prayer:

Satan, I command you to loose my harvest in the Name of Jesus. I forbid you to interfere, hinder or delay its coming in Jesus name. I curse every assignment you have sent against it. I bind every hindering spirit, every spirit of delay coming against my harvest.

I loose my harvest in Jesus' name. I speak to every mountain standing in the way of my harvest being delivered to into my hand to be rooted up and to be cast into the sea in Jesus' name.

Pray this prayer with authority. Pray in faith knowing God is releasing your harvest.

Again, like all the other prayers in this book, this prayer is simply a guide. The Holy Spirit will give further instructions in prayer if it is necessary. The devil is under your feet and must obey you, so boldly loose your harvest!

Chapter Fourteen
Be Diligent

The lazy man does not roast what he took in hunting, but diligence is man's precious possession. ***Proverbs 12:27***

One thing being with Jesus has taught me, He put me in a position where I would have to be diligent to achieve my dreams. This is particularly true for those of us who have been living from paycheck to paycheck. You know deep down in your spirit there is more, but what effort will you make to achieve it?

The average individual will just talk about how good things could be or rather complain about the situation. But God has given us all the tools we need to acquire wealth: His Word, His power, His anointing, His grace, His goodness, His kindness, and among other things, His mercy.

When I was living paycheck to paycheck, I purposed in my heart because Jesus had delivered me from the curse of poverty, I was not going to settle for being poor.

Consider the Jesus' parable in *Matthew 25:14-21*

[14]For it is like a man who was about to take a long journey, and he called his servants together and entrusted them with his property.

[15]To one he gave five talents [probably about $5,000], to another two, to another one – to each in proportion to his own personal ability. Then he departed and left the country.

[16]He who had received the five talents went at once and traded with them, and he gained five talents more.

[17]And likewise he who had received the two talents- he also gained two talents more.

[18]But he who had received the one talent went and dug a hole in the ground and hid his master's money.

[19]Now after a long time the master of those servants returned and settled accounts with them.

[20]And he who had received the five talents came and brought him five more saying, Master, you entrusted to me five talents; see, here I have gained five talents more.

[21]His master said to him, Well done, you upright (honorable, admirable) and faithful servant! You have been faithful and trustworthy over a little; I will put you in charge of much. Enter into and share the joy which your master enjoys.

The moral of the story is: God has placed within each of us talents and giftings. Some of those giftings have the ability to bless us and to create wealth for the kingdom of God. We are responsible for using those talents and gifting; and we will be held accountable for "sitting on them."

In addition to using our natural talents and abilities, we should be diligent in prayer, in seeking God and our tithing and giving.

At the beginning of this book, I stated that all things do work together for the good of those who love God and who are called according to His purpose.

II Peter 1:10
"Wherefore the rather, brethren, give diligence to make your calling and election sure: for if you do these things, ye shall never fail."

Peter, in this scripture, is talking about attaining spiritual things. He is saying to us when one responds in faith to the promises of God, he receives the divine gift of new life, but even this involves diligence on our part. How much more earthly things like our finances? In my opinion, the lowest form of blessing is a job. Consider the following scriptures:

II Thessalonians 3:6-10
[6]Now we charge you, brethren, in the name of Jesus Christ (the Messiah) that you withdraw and keep away from every brother (fellow believer) who is slack in the performance of duty and is disorderly, living as a shirker and not walking in accord with the traditions and instructions that you have received from us.
[7]For yourselves know how it is necessary to imitate or example, for we were with you [we were not idle].
[8]Nor did we eat anyone's bread without paying for it, but with toil and struggle we worked night and day, that we might not be broken.

[9] [It was] not because we do not have a right [to such support], but [we wished] to make ourselves an example for you to follow.

[10] For while we were yet with you, we gave you this rule *and* charge: If anyone will not work, neither let him eat.

Paul, in these passages of scripture is talking about being idle. I personally believe that toil came because of the Fall of Adam. However, I believe that God uses work to prepare us, train us and inspire us to seek Him for all the abundance that His kingdom has to offer.

There were many days I sat at an office desk and dreamed of being financially self-sufficient. In my own heart I knew that there was more. Not just more money, but more freedom to pursue things that God had put in my heart for the Kingdom.

I wanted to do these things, attend conferences, go learn more about spiritual gifts and so on, but it was my responsibility to my job that kept me from doing these things.

But thank God, diligence in studying God's Word, confessing the Word about my prosperity caused a change in my financial situation!

Chapter Fifteen
Don't Let Go of Your Faith

*As for the rich in this world, charge them not to be proud and arrogant and contemptuous of others, not to set their hopes on uncertain riches, but on God, Who richly and ceaselessly provides us with everything for [our] enjoyment. **I Timothy 6:17***

A few months after God blessed me, I went on a ten day vacation on the other side of the country. I was very excited about going because I was going to attend a Christian conference. I had never had the financial ability to pay the expenses to go on a trip like this before. I wasted no time in registering. The conference was in Los Angeles, California.

As a result of this trip, God taught me a lesson I would never forget. The lesson was: you may have money in the bank, but you still need your faith in God. Just before leaving for California, I had lost my credit card and had run out of checks at the same time. I said to myself "no problem will just carry enough cash for any other expenses I had not anticipated."

My trip was divided into two parts. I was supposed to depart Augusta, Georgia and catch a flight a week later for Los Angeles, out of Little Rock, Arkansas.

I was unable to catch the flight out of Augusta, Georgia due to some things that had come up. Changing my itinerary was going to cost me over a thousand dollars. Instead I thought I would just get on the bus and arrive in Little Rock, Arkansas just in time to depart for Los Angeles.

After arriving in Little Rock, Arkansas on Friday afternoon, I settled into my hotel room. About ten o'clock that night, the Holy Spirit that prompted me to contact the airline to see how far in advance I would have to arrive before departure. The airline agent informed me my whole itinerary had been cancelled the day I failed to arrive in Augusta, Georgia for that flight. I was devastated. I could not believe this was happening to me. Here I was in the middle of the country and my ticket reservation to California had been cancelled.

So without a hesitation I called the bus station because I was determined to arrive on Saturday as planned. I wanted to attend services on Sunday there in the city. I called my sister to tell her what had happened. She had gone through this type of situation before and her exact words to me were: "Girl, if I were you, I would use my faith and go to that airport anyway."

At first I shuttered at the thought of this. I told her I will do it if you touch and agree with me that God will part the waters for me. My faith was in the prayer of agreement.

Matthew 18:19
Again, I tell you, if two of you on earth (harmonize together, make a symphony together) about whatever [anything and everything] they may ask, it will come to pass and be done for them by My Father in heaven.

My faith was wholly in this scripture. It had worked for me hundreds of times during my Christian life. I knew if we touched and agreed in prayer about it, according to the Word, God would honor it.

I would have to admit, I was very nervous all night and I did sleep well. I determined I was going to get on the plane and if this was true, I would have to miss the bus leaving for Los Angeles at around 5:00am too. Faith always involves some type of risk. I made the decision to trust God and miss my opportunity to catch the bus. Finally, at about 3:00 am, I got up and just started praising the Lord. A spirit of thanksgiving came upon me and I began to laugh. I lay down in peace, knowing I had the victory!

At 5:00am, I awakened and got up, showered and left for the airport. I was still a little apprehensive, but the majority of what I was feeling was peace. It was what I call the confirmation and affirmation of the Holy Spirit. It was the peace of God that surpasses all understanding.

Once I arrived at the airport I went to the counter and I told the reservation clerk my name. I also told her I was to leave for Los Angeles at 7:50. She looked up my reservation and immediately she told me my ticket had been cancelled.

I played the stupid for a second, but then I began to ask her was there anything she could do to help me get to Los Angeles. I was actually hoping she would hit a magic button and reinstate my itinerary.

She was quick to tell me there was nothing she could do. I asked for the manager to submit my request to him. He looked at me and said there was nothing to be done as well. Again, I was shattered and even though I remained very polite, I was somewhat angry. I was angry with my sister for even suggesting I come to the airport in the first place; angry with the Lord for allowing me to be in this situation and angry with myself for skipping the initial flight out of Augusta, Georgia.

In quiet surrender, I gathered my bags and headed for the outside doors. I stood there for a moment to gather my thoughts. By choosing to walk by faith and go to the airport, I had missed the next bus to Los Angeles and another would not be leaving for another six hours.

Just as I was about to leave through the doors, the reservation attendant who had informed me of my ticket cancellation, came running towards me. She said, "Ms. Sanders, we can get you to Los Angeles and back to Augusta for $755.00." This was music to my ears because I was told by the reservations agent on my initial attempt to change my itinerary it would cost me $2,300.00!

All the money I had in my possession was $800.00. I had seen God come through for me. I knew He would continue to do so long as I trusted Him. Please take note: I had thousands in my bank account, but it did not do me any good because I could not access it. I had to continue use my faith!

After I paid for my airplane ticket, I phoned my sister to tell her the news. She said she had meant to pay her car note earlier in the week, but had been extremely busy and was unable to do so. She said she would send $400.00 to help pay the $200.00 per night lodging for three days.

I also remembered I had my ATM card and I could withdraw $250.00. However, I would only be able to withdraw this amount once. The machines would register this withdrawal the entire weekend, preventing me from withdrawing any more money until Monday morning.

Upon my arrival in Los Angeles, I paid for the lodging, leaving me with $50.00 until Monday morning. I wanted to attend services, but I had to catch a cab. Cabs can be very expensive in Los Angeles. I had to pray and call on the Lord.

God is a good, good God! He had enabled me to get to Los Angeles on the plane, avoiding a two to three day ride on the bus. I had paid for my lodging; I had made it to church and back. I had money for dinner and all I had to do was make it to Monday. Praise God! He showed me my money in the bank hadn't done me any good.

It was my faith in Him that had given me the victory in the situation. My brothers and sisters, don't let go your faith when your wealth comes!

ABOUT THE AUTHOR

Dr. Linda Sharon Sanders is an ordained minister with an MBA in Business and Global Finance. Currently she hosts a broadcast on blogtalkeradio.com as the Dream Interpreter. She has always believed Jesus preached the Gospel to the poor so they could be free from poverty and step into the abundance that He provided for them. So escaping poverty is not only a matter of your education or family status, but it is a matter of obedience to God and knowing how to implement Kingdom of God principles. Dr. Sanders believes Jesus meant for every man to be able to overcome poverty, just as He meant for every man to overcome sickness, sin and spiritual death.

This book details her initial encounter with supernatural finance and how she obtained her first supernatural harvest. She credits the Kingdom of God because she created it with nothing but the words of her mouth and kingdom principles.

www.ingramcontent.com/pod-product-compliance
Lightning Source LLC
Chambersburg PA
CBHW060122050426
42448CB00010B/1991